DEATH OF

Simon Zec writes poems on his phone to put in a notebook so he can read them out to people and look like a proper poet. Now he has his own proper book to read them out from.

Based in Steyning in West Sussex, he works with trees and writes poems to vent his spleen about life, politics and his easy life.

Death of the Suburb

To Christine + Tom

Love to you!

Si Bec

Simon ~~Zec~~

THE REAL PRESS

www.therealpress.co.uk

Published in 2018 by the Real Press.
www.therealpress.co.uk
© Simon Zec

ISBN (print) 9781912119561
ISBN (ebooks) 9781912119554

For Bean, Kip and Fab.
Without you, I wouldn't have the support, space or inspiration.

And for Mum; who knows what you would have thought of all this.

Introduction

After a long decade of ignoring the written word, I found myself in a quiet space the day after a friend's funeral.

Sat watching the Downs, a poem came out. Then a few more came out again.

Hooking up with the Norfolk Arms-based Raz-up folk, I found a space to inflict these words on people. From there the words grew and flooded out.

Without the support of Bean, allowing me to mid-life crisis like a whirling dervish, whilst she steadfastly trusted me and just let me get on with it, I would be nowhere.

My fellow Razzmaticians have allowed me to chuck words around and humour me whilst nailing my feet to the floor.

Thanks to Rich, I have had someone to follow and evolve with, just a while after he has.

Thanks to Sara the bookshop queen, who has always been wonderfully supportive.

Without David expanding his publishing empire to a poetry wing, my dream of this book would still be piping.

Thanks also to Julie (2), the pub crawl poets, the Mollies and all the other folk who've actually treated me like a poet as opposed to whatever I actually feel like.

And finally to Kip and Fab, without whom I wouldn't have half as much inspiration to be who I want to be, or be awake so early to find the time to write.

Death of the suburb

The place where I grew up has turned to shit.

It was so smart and clean.
So suburban and green.

Now it's busy and confusing and noisy and dirty.
Full of emptiness and mourning and sorrow and fear.

The streets don't shine anymore.
The people don't smile anymore.

My house is someone else's. A shrine. A mausoleum.

It was so nice and easy.
Nothing to write about really.
Now it's full of so much dirt it could make a thousand
    fucking poems.

We and you

We're the ones with no legal aid
We're the ones with over-crowded classrooms
We're the ones queuing in the hospital
We're the ones waiting for the appointment for months
We're the ones waiting at the train stations

You can idealise and theorise and austeritise as much as
    you want
You can cut and cut and cut till it's making a profit
You can sell off and privatise in the name of savings
You can argue and spin it all till it all makes sense in your
    head

But

We're the ones queuing at the food banks
We're the ones not getting any pay rises
We're the ones being lied to on the sides of buses
We're the ones who can't afford a house
We're the ones getting ploughed into
We're the ones burning in our flats
We're the ones being blown up

You're the ones telling us there's more money available
You're the ones telling us it's someone else's fault
You're the ones telling us it's for the best

4

You're the ones telling us you care

But

We're the ones getting angrier and angrier
We're the ones who will rise up
We're the ones who will not take it anymore
We're the ones who will realise that it's our world and we
    want it back

And you'll be the ones who will have to give it up
Because together we are the 98 per cent
And there's more of us
And we will unite
And we will stand tall
And we won't take it anymore

Gluck

It was one of those close Steyning nights
six days into threatening a storm
But holding out, making us sweat for a few more days
Before it reluctantly dribbles down about four hydrogens
and a couple of pathetic oxygens
The room was full of poets and air and too many celcius's
Words rumbled and tumbled and flowed and growed
I wanted to mock or run screaming from the room for fear
of being too middle aged or middle class or middle of the
    fucking road
But I stayed and waited patiently for my turn
Flipping poems in my head
My blood pumped in anticipation
The release released
Breathed out
Vented
To take the compliments and flip them back to the next
    poeter
Mutually assured backscratchen
Walking home writing on my phone
Spewing out some self reflection
Ready for the next one

The problem with poetry

The problem with poetry is
Other People's Poems.
Listening to them bare they're soul
Or hear their every fucking thought

I'm only here so you can hear
My fantastic creation
To spread my words
Of amazing imagination

The problem with poetry
Is listening to all this shit
From him and her and him
And her and her and him

Going on and on about this thing
Metaphors and analogies stretched so thin
A full room of poets, waiting for the cue to clap
Wondering how they got from there to that

The problem with poetry is clear
All of us have found the time to make it to here
And even in the weirdest longest oddest of them all
There's a place of beauty
a spot of truth
Where no rhyme is wrong

No way is wrong
With passion and humour
And bare boned honesty

And, from a scrap of paper,
Or
A beautifully bound book,
Or
A phone
Or
For some clever soul, their memory

And from this place, this chrysallis, a beautiful butterfly
    flutters out
Lands on my nose
And pokes me in the eye

Hanging by a bed

My bowels and head were fighting for supremacy
One dragging me up the other forcing me deeper
I was left suspended in deanimation
Neither asleep nor awake
Hanging by a bed

The sounds from last night knocking on my ears
Memories of laughs and lines and smiles
Searching the blanks for any need of regret
Wondering if I need to apologise

The stockpiled pretzels diminished in one night
The stack of multi shaped glasses ready to be washed
The recycling bin brimmed full

Stomach lined with greasy carbs
Then emptied again
Double double espresso
The brain clears enough to start the day

The hottest day of the year

The sun shone on the green green grass
Cows ruminated around
Speeding up and moving around
With no logic or reason to be perceived
And Adam Buxton poured Brian Eno another cup of tea
To discuss writing pop songs in the first person plural

Washing hanging on the line
Work clothes preparing themselves for the week ahead
The roof runners of suburbia run from shed to shed to
    trampoline
The whites and pinks and blossoms drifting to the ground
    in the breeze
Children planning the world and sneaking off to the
    hammock with another snack

The buds bursting open and we all go out to join them
Sunnies on. Shorts out. Tees shirted
Someone somewhere is walking a dog
A cat lazily stalks some invisible thing

The air is filled with birds and flies and pollen and
    butterflies
Whatever pathetic excuse for a cloud there is in the sky
    drifts past
No one anywhere is doing anything they have to do

As the sun approaches the horizon
The beer and wine escapes their bottles into our brains
And the day turns to night
Our skin reddened by unpreparedness and fun
And we sleep wherever we land
Dream dreams of the summer to come
To awake late with thick heads
And dry mouths
Ready for another day just like this

Global herd mentality

You can give them views and friends and freedoms
You can give the freesat and internet tele
You can limit the time they play on computers
But wherever you do
However you try to control it
Some fucker on a YouTube channel will sneak on a swears
Or some innocent looking game will turn out to involve
multiple bloody killings of a rag doll

You can teach them to live and be kind and respect
Say please and thank you wherever they're a guest
But whatever you do
However you train them
They'll be inundated with societal norms
And TV shows with a beefed up bloke and waif like girl
And they'll revert to the gender stereotypes that society
    demands.

This global herd mentality
This wild wild web
Will drag them into the new centre ground.
We've given our child minding over to the internet
It used to be only the adverts on tiny pop plus one to watch
    out for
With McDonald's promoting its milk and carrots in the
    happy meal

But now it's some bloke with a microphone filming himself
    playing some game
Which links to the next one and the next one
Until it spirals down until they're watching someone sniper
a crowd of protesters
And it's a laugh
And the graphics get so good that in ten years time we can
watch someone Facebook live doing it for real
And we'll still laugh
Cos we would have lost the ability to demarcate

And we'll blame t'internet
Or we'll blame Google
Or we'll blame the *Daily Mail*
Or we'll blame one religion or another
But it's all of our faults
We all let it happen
And we'll say there's nothing we can do
And we've been worn down to it
And I'm sure it'll be broadly fine
Broadly

Portrait of a man

He spoke into his phone like he was in *The Apprentice*
But he wasn't. Far from it
He could hardly keep his business together
Let alone keep his wife and kids happy
His hair was jauntily long
And coiffed like he gave too much of a toss
Everyone was 'matey' or 'gov'nor'
But mainly cos he couldn't be arsed to remember their
    names
He wore sunglasses.
Not to hide his eyes
But to cover up his staring at women's breasts.
When he's at Legoland Windsor be pays to jump the queue
    Not noticing the angry stares from the poor sods having
    queued for fifty minutes to get to where his money has
    got him
On birthdays he takes his mum to Smith and Western for a
    steak and chips
His mum pays
He spits at the homeless when he's drunk
In a father and child tennis match, he'll make sure all his
    shots are at the kid.
He'll buy his son an iPhone 7 for his fifth birthday
But it's OK,
Cos he's got a T7 camper van
And he's good at football

A rhymy poem

Nationwide can show us a rhymy poem
About how great if it's to have a house to own
But how the hell are we supposed to do that?
No deposit. No income. Waiting to inherit?

And how the hell are the future lot
Riddled with debt and exorbitant costs
Supposed to be the ones who'll own
If there isn't a chance nationwide will really loan?

With no careers or pension there
And parental houses sold to pay for their care

With the only housing available
Being there for one and all
If you have a deposit of 100 grand
And earn 70k per annum

No council housing left for those in need
Sold and sold for the market to feed
So the ladders so fucking high up
Unobtainable for those with no luck

Stuck with rent twice the cost of a mortgage
Leaving only enough for those to manage

So you can fill our hearts with twee little rhymes
But the reality doesn't rhyme or look to end
It sucks and only looks like it's getting worse

The vacant stare of the aristocrat

Red-jeaned and g and t'd,
With a vacant stare from years of not having to worry too
    much about anything
Luxuriously shabbied vehicles driving down the cedar lined
    driveway
To a house too expensive to renovate and too big to fail
Educated to the highest degree means they have the skills
    and ability to get on with everyone.
Not needing to prove their class by belittling the little ones
Not needing to cover up their accent in shame for they are
    shamelessly proud
No fear of revolution or change.
Because the rest of us have been trained into subjugation
Like film stars we subconsciously cowtow
Because their Christian charity may be bestowed upon one
    of our plans
They are the crocodiles of our class system.
Unchanged and prehistoric.
Everyone is so friendly to them, listening to their stories at
    the bar at night.
Privileged seats at the school play
Privileged parts for the kids
Innocently living this way for they know not what they do
The bias is my bias
My crippling leftism blinkers my view
Hating myself for my attitude

They shit like I do
They hide quietly in the dark
They drink to forget
They worry
Some of them are actually nice people

The people of Aleppo

The people of Aleppo found that meme you shared hilarious. Could you share it on their timeline please? Might cheer them up.

The people of Aleppo were wondering what your year looked like? Have you got a quick photo montage for them to look at?

The people of Aleppo were fascinated by that maths quiz. Might give them something to think about whilst they're being murdered as they try to escape their burning town

The people of Aleppo were wondering what you had for dinner? Got any picture proof?

The people of Aleppo were just thinking about how you spent your night. Did you Facebook live it by any chance?

The people of Aleppo were just asking where their flags were on your Facebook profile?

The people of Aleppo were really glad you shared that video about that MP saying our government wasn't doing enough to help out the people of Aleppo

The people of Aleppo are waiting with baited breath for
your next angry poem

The people of Aleppo
The people of Aleppo
The people of Aleppo
The people of Aleppo
The people of Aleppo

I'm a Jew

I am a Jew
Though I'm don't feel very Jewish
I am a dad
But I don't often act responsibly
I am English
But I don't feel very patriotic
I am a Londoner
But I haven't lived in London for years
I am a Steyningite
But sometimes I don't feel I belong
I am a poet
But I don't often rhyme

Leonard Cohen's poem

How can Leonard Cohen write such a short poem?
How can what he say be said so easily?
Did he sweat those words?
Did they come like water from a tap?
Or were they like a tree grown in the woods?

What makes his short concise beautifying thoughts?
How come that it is what it is?
I could write one so quick
Might be as good too.

Dead trees

These retirees all pensioned up
With time on their hands
Wandering to buy them at the shops

Dispersed amongst commuters to fill their journey
To stop them talking or thinking
Indoctrination subliminally from the intestine of the
   Daily Mail

Given air time by the news
As if it represents your views
This small elite chip away at our souls

The vested interested owners
Off shored and on side
Capitalistically, unelectedly making our views

The dead trees dying daily to less and fewer
But still they're forced into a printing press
And given so much power

After bringing down governments
And setting up celebs
Trying to anger us to action

Their hypocrisy knows no bounds
Their influence unhindered
And we buy them nonetheless

Soon they will be no more
As less and less will be able to retire
And everyone's online

We can read from so many different sources
That their influence will disperses
And the trees can breathe a sigh of relief

Wwwdotters

Slavered in lacquer and lycra
High waists and I-plugs in ears
Over made up and slanging on their phones
Drinking choca mocha locha fochas

muscled and power shaked up
Sliding right or left after a quick judgemental judgement
Instagramised and comatosed from call of duty and porn

We thought we had it bad
high rents and overpriced houses
Student loans and growing up under Thatcher
Us generation Xers have done our fun
And settled down into breeding and binge drinking
With the occasional puff and rare big night out at the
football club

The ones before settled into retirement with their pension
and post career life
Wandering to town to buy the *Mail* in the morning
Volunteering and looking after the community
With their job for life and long drawn out third age

Whereas these millennium kids
These generation wwwdotters
Know immediacy

4ging or WiFi coding their way to knowledge
They don't need calculators or watches
Or books or tele
They've been gamified and apped
Their lives are on demand
They are in control of it all

Their reality is so virtual to be true
But the reality of their future is so vague
No houses
No careers
No way to keep the lights on
No privacy

They are astronauts to the future pioneers into this new
    world
Finding their way cos we cannot lead them
We have no idea how to guide them
We're strangers to this world
We've been caught between books and ipads
Between vinyl and mp3s
We remember Somerfields
To them it's only ever been Co-op
What can we tell them?

Not on the ladder

I'm not on the ladder
I'm in a rut
Stuck in a loop
But its spiralling out

We've got to start again
Got to change our life
To upheavalise
Without going mad

Cos I wasted my youth
With frivolity and moments
Not planning for the future
Cos I didn't have one

Bumbling from job to no job
From experience to experience
Stunted my life
For a swim in the ocean

And now life is catching up with me
Responsibility waves his ugly flag
And I have nothing
Just blind hope

Giving up booze

The strange shape next to my bed
Stared at me as I awoke
A stack of light up Lego bricks
Pretending to be disorrano.

The opened bottle of wine calls to me
Sat on the fridge pleading to be finished
Looking for a glass to fill to the brim
And be quaffed in front of the fire

The bottles of ale hidden in a cupboard
Pushes the door ajar and shows a hint of side
If It wiggles its hips enough
It'll get put in a pint glass

The minute I open the door
After working for a bit
Or walking past the pub
Or queuing in Somerfield
Or the kids are a bit annoying
Or I've got to do another job
Or the phone keeps on ringing
Or I'm about to start the washing up
Or its time to cook the Sunday lunch
Or a friend has come to visit
Or I've played a game of football

Or the kids are in the park
Or I'm in a pub
Or a restaurant
Or a café
Or a beach
Or a picnic

It's not that I drink to forget
I don't drink to get drunk
I don't blackout very often
I don't even drink to excess, much

I'll stop after two or three
Sometimes after just one
But the bottle in my head
Pleads to be refilled every day

It's no nebuchadnezzar
Not even a magnum
Just a beautiful pewter tankard
Pleading to be of use

But now I'm trying to resist it
Ask it to quieten down for a while
To show it I can ignore it
And that makes it shout louder still

It grows arms to tap my shoulder
And bangs a big bass drum as I come home
But I'll cut its arms off
Kick the big bass drum out of its way
Smash it into tiny pieces
And feed it to itself

And one day soon it'll be quietened
Submissed into silence
And it'll be under my control
And the beautiful pewter tankard will be happily stored in
    a cupboard

My privilege and place

I have no right as a first world white male.
I shouldn't be upset or offended by a rape case being
    turned around.
By the use of previous history of sexual behaviour by a
    victim to prove a perpetrator's innocence.
There is no real reason why I should care

And I have no right to have an opinion on whether it's right
    or true.
To be offended that the victim had been named.
Or that the accused should have a right to anonymity.
I shouldn't demand that he should be named.

I have no reason to care about the millionth person killed
    by a bomb
Dropped on an town in the middle of a country thousands
    of miles away from where I live.
My privilege and place mean I shouldn't give a toss.

And I don't need to care that anther black man was shot
In a small part of the States just because of his race

And I shouldn't care if a man makes a derogatory comment
    about a woman
If only other men hear it

Or a person says something racist
If everyone around is white

And I may not deal with these situations perfectly.
Every time that I experience them
And my anger and fear as I hear these things.
Shouldn't be so extreme

But I am and I do and I will and I should
And I can't stop it
But I can fight it

And my privilege and place
Gives me the power to face
Up to the situation
Gives me the tools to fight it

And if I look and see
To use my empathy
Beyond the comfy town
In a comfy county
In a comfy country
In a lucky place
Born with a lucky face

So all I can do is as much as I can
By talking and sharing.
And confronting (if I'm brave enough)
And by teaching my children.

To pass on to them the revolutionary spirit
To not give up the fight
To change the injustice
Because one day
It may be them
Who will have so much power that they
Might have chance to change the world

Or stop a war
Or simply treat strangers with love and respect
Treat everyone as equals

Or simply my boys may be in a situation where they could
take advantage
Of a drunk girl
But they choose not to
And to be honest
That would be enough

I want to lie in

I want to lie in like I was 16 again
Just lie in bed close my eyes and sleep –
To drift past midday.

I wish my caffeine addled brain
Would take the morning off,
and some of the afternoon too;

To go back to the time when my body,
So naive and independent,
Didn't need to evacuate first thing on the morning.

I've no need to be up so early
Apart from needing to feed
And getting to work

I don't want to see the best part of the day
I don't want to photograph that golden hour
I want to wake up and have no idea what time it is

I wish my body didn't ache me awake
My back straightening me back to the world
The cares in the world so burdensome

John Humphrys and Mishal Husain
Can chat on without me.

I don't want to hear about cities burning
Or how intelligent horses are

I'd rather just stew in a duvet
And snooze passed two

I don't want to get up a spend an hour quietly writing
I want to piss it away unconscious,
Snoring and dribbling on to a pillow.

Wowo

There are no secrets in a field full of people -
Everything is heard and seen.
You can surround yourself with the comforts of home
Whilst watching the stars

You can turn up in your T5.5
All tooled up looking cool
In your low-slung jeans
And your Tibeten T.
But in the morning we'll find you in your tiger onesie
queueing for a poo at 7:42

Drinking in the afternoon is fine,
if the kids are safely out of ear shot
Covered in mud and bruises.
Whilst you are in thick fog of an English sparkling wine

Rich and poor
All classes United under Canvas
Kids mingling like they have no idea what Marx ever wrote
    about

Some idiot uncle feels the need to engage the children,
Trying to impress everyone with his fun personality
Whilst the rest of us hope for another ten minutes of
    ignoring

before nursing their cuts and quarrels and rumbling
    stomachs

The childless couple surrounded by screams and needs,
Pretending it's OK,
But secretly planning their escape

Popping to the barn and back
To rejenga the fridge to get to your butter
And wander back to your spot,
Nodding hellos and having a quick chat about your night's
    sleep or the latest camping gadget.

If you're desperate after four days, you have to leave camp
    and head off to Tescos
Forced to interact with your children and the neon reality.
It's enough to drive you mildly insane.

Back home to the tent and the warm comfort of an
afternoon beer eases the soul and resets the brain.
Feed the kids and light the fire
Re-assemble at the teepee for candlelit serenades

Dragging the bag-eyed children forcing them to bed
sitting around the firepit
crocs slowly melting
Whilst your back is damp and cold
And off to bed to start the day with a hangover and cup of
    warm caffeine.

To repeat and repeat for as long as you can get away with
Squeezing an extra night or two until the weather or the
money runs out

The bow-legged rich man

He was a bow-legged rich man
With a couple of spoilt-rotten kids
His wife will sit and read the *Times*
As he cowboyed around the camp like a posh Clint
    Eastwood

In his silk pyjamas and expensive sandles,
They'll eat duchy of Cornwall sausages
On the travel bar-b-q.

He'll provide the best for his family
Defend them with all his off-shored might

One of his spoilt little children starts and loses a fight
With a little raggamuffin

The spoilt little child
With his bow legs in training,
Struts to his dad and with his weakest voice
Tells the bow-legged rich man of the raggamuffin's badness

The bow-legged rich man will be over to the little
raggamuffin's raggamuffin parents

With His entitled bonhomie
He Will force these poor innocent raggamuffin's

raggamuffin parents
To make the raggamuffin, unfairly chastised, to apologise
    to the spoilt little child
And the raggamuffin's raggamuffin parents will have to
apologise too

And the spoilt little child
Learnt to harness the power of The bow-legged rich man
And the raggamuffin learnt his place

And the bow-legged rich man
The gap between his legs
As wide as his confidence
Will strut back to his bell tent
And read his paper
And drink a lovely g and t

Whilst the spoilt little child
Goes back to the hordes of children
And prepares for his next fight

Kip

You fill up so much of my eyes as I watch you sleep,
With your blue blue eyes and your mop of hair
I can only guess what is going on in your brain
As you stare into space and wiggle your fingers.

You used to be so dependant
Jigsawed onto my shoulder to sleep
Waking every hour to be Paul Wellered to sleep.

You transformed our lives
Taught us to make a new life trained us to be parents

Making friends in a millisecond
Keeping them for ages

Your confidence and politeness make me fill to the brim
    with pride

Everytime you sneeze and sneeze and sneeze and sneeze
    and sneeze
I see my mum again
And for the first time in my life, it is not conflicted.
You've brought me light

As you grow and go
I want you to know

We've done our best

And you've taken it,
Absorbed it and made an amazing you.

Whatever tree you choose to be
Your roots are strong
And nourished with love
And we'll always be there for you
Anyways care for you
Always have you back

The red crested swallow

A heron stills in a field as the green green canal reflects the
    evening sun
It stands neutrally waiting till its the right time to feed
The buzzards skreetch overhead, hiding behind the trees
The ancient oaks and the ashes stretch
A single bleating lamb calls for its mother
The siblings chat on the poop deck
Whiling away the hours, contemplating the flowers
    consulting with the birds
The last bridge approaches to dock and part after a week to
    always remember.
Sleeping in cramped noisy parts of a boat you wouldn't
    think is sleepable.

Pootling along, chatting, betting and eating.
A dad dadding children too old to be dadded
The children letting their dadding dad on cos he's their dad
The youngsters feeding ducks or playing games or doing
    what they want.
This golden idyll in a golden age on a golden canal boat in a
    golden time.

The wharf approaches for us to jump into action one last
    time
Before we part till Christmas
With hugs and tears

And memories and photos and laughs to remember.
Twas a surprisingly good holiday
Immersed in beauty and tranquillity.

Aber g llan nyg dud

People dredged along by life in a town ruined by Tescos.
The pubs boarded up and emptied by the 3 for 10 pounds
     wine at the Co-op petrol shop
Shop fronts hidden by the circus adverts,
with their two for one deal on a Tuesday afternoon
Charity shops and tea houses interspersed with *maison
     vert* and boutiqueries is all that's left or new.

The pre teens with their high waists in their white jeans
Selfieing themselves outside Martin's the newsagents
The crack thin mums smoking a fag whilst the dad eats a
     pack of Starmix
Shouting across to the opposite bus stop making plans for
curry and a pint in the generic bargain pub with a name
I'm too depressed to remember

A china cup drops from a charity shop bag and smashes on
     the road
The bus queue mutters disapproval at the embarrassed
     rushed job of clearing up

The two-for-one happy hour extends to a happy month in
the desperate hope of keeping the pub from the grasping
tentacles of the big four
Hoping to cement their hierarchy by destroying the Spar
     shop on the corner

Everyone moans about the death of their town as they
Amazon the costs and click and collect
Comparing the price of a banana and having a safe place to
leave the future of the town
As the bus defiantly gets later and delayder
The queue gets longer and longer
We would have had time to write a postcard, with a picture
of the town when it was as poor as it is now, but cuter
cos it was in sepia then.
But no need to buy the postcard from the shop and use a
stamp as we have an app that for free p and p
we can instagram our faces on a scene

do it all on the free wiFi in the café where we used the loo.

The bus finally comes.
Stuffed to standing as we mooch back to our boat for our
last night in an industrial past.
As we glide back to the cars for a long drive home first
thing in the morning.
The kids quietened and subdued by iplayer downloads
as we GPS, mobile data and Google our way home.
Back to work, back to life, back to our cosy town.

I've gone on holiday to the 1970s

I've gone on holiday to the 1970s,
Where men drink beer and read the paper
The women do the washing and the washing up
And make the tea.
The kettle must be boiled from the top for every cup

We are in that crossover point for feminism
We've reached the part where both sides know it's
    unsustainable
But we're going to keep at it for as long as possible
Us men are enjoying the situation
And the women only seem to complain about it without
    actually not doing it.

The cars are driven by the men
And the dishwasher is emptied by us
And one of us takes the rubbish out
So when we're told we do nothing we have these pathetic
excuses for effort as evidence.

We're told we drink too much and we say 'I'm on holiday'.
We're off fishing for the day
And the ladies are off shopping
And thinking about dinner

Us men play at being kids again

Whilst our tea is made for us
From that over-filled kettle
Boiling away the environment a kilowatt hour at a time

And everything is left on charge overnight
And salad is some cos lettuce and a fat tasteless tomato

My lactose intolerance has just disappeared
And nothing, simply nothing is gluten free

Low impact parenting

What I'm doing is empowering the children
Low impact parenting
Encouraging self reliance
By giving them the freedom,
they're learning to self stim

I've got half a half an eye on them
I'm there if they need me
Trusting them to be themselves
Waiting to intervene

Meanwhile I'm allowing myself some down time
A break from all this empowering
Thinking about stuff
Is extraordinarily tiring

The world won't get saved by poetry,
on its own
And the political system won't be brought down without
me half reading and then sharing it on Facebook
if I'm busy interacting with non-voting children;

When one of them falls over,
I'll check if their histerics are histrionic
Or if I genuinely need to panic
If it is, I'll be there as quick as I can

Once my phone is safely in a pocket

And then I'll cuddle them and reassure them
And get them back on their feet.
Send them off with a reassuring pat on the bum
And go back to my seat.

I'm preparing them for adulthood
Learning to be alone
Coping with the outside world
And modelling being on the phone

The confusing tube

The tube hadn't changed
The people seem the same

Just now everyone looks at their phones instead of their
shoes

Or they read a paper that is free to them
But comes with the blood of a thousand *Daily Mail*s

Ingesting their bile and hatred
Disguised in mediocrity

Or you can go online
For the price of your email to be sold and digested and
turned into advertising sushi,

As we indehiscently absorb the modern world,

Not knowing what we let ourselves into but not caring
cos it's FREE

The click click of the rails replaced by the tick tick of the
headphones from another apple phone

I used to revel in breaking the conventions of the London
    underground

Putting my feet up on the seats
Leaving interesting books on random seats
Travelling to funny named stations
Now it's head down and try and work out the ticketing
    system,

Waiting for friends at the exit like a teenager because
they're not organised enough to turn up ten minutes early.

My teenaged self would write more pretentious poetry.
With words people wouldn't understand to try and impress
then with my knowledge.
I'm better than that now.

I don't rhyme so much now.
My need to impress is so much more tantric nowadays
I don't need the approval of these random strangers on a
    tube.
I can wait till is read out at a much larger date.

Coming back to a city that was once home
Is no longer my time -
I've shrunk away from it
Isolated myself from its diversity.
And now I'm a small town boy in a small town world

Parchment in a palace

It was all supposed to be over in 1997 -
Years and years of fighting and rebelling.
We could all take our feet off the pedal,
Sit back and enjoy the ride

We didn't need to fight any more.
We have reclaimed our society -
The train spotters, the levellers and pulp
had finally won the war.

By partying and slacking, we changed the world
So to celebrate, we partied like it was 1999
And we kept on partying
Harder than ever.
The millennium bug came and went.
We started to eat meat again,
cos finally you could get a decent veggie option in a café.
Our laurels were so well rested
You would hardly know we were there.

Then we just settled down.
Amnesty international carried on without us,
Chuggers took over the streets
And giving to charity was a form away from direct debits -
No need to campaign:
We had labelled paid volunteers getting a commission on

everyone they sign up -
commoditised donating

Soon families came along,
Spare time became sparse time.
No time to worry about the world:
I had kids to worry over instead
The world was fine.
We left it well-looked after last time I checked

Then the bloody internet came about
With phones that could easily remind us of what's gone
     wrong
And now all we can see is the mess we left behind.
Apparently, whoever was looking after our world
didn't seem to carry on with our plans.
They may have slightly let the side down,
And now we have to start all over again

But I'm too old now to fight -
I'm not sure I have the strength to do it.
We need the next gen to take over,
But their brains might be too full of instagram and porn
Speedy trite solutions to an easily accessible world

But the cogs and controls are still on parchment in a palace
The digital revolution has sped on
So what hope is there?

Oh God, it is all so fucked.
We have to do something
But I'm at a loss at what to do.

Please advise.

Cannabis Chris

He was a tough man with a tiny dog,
As if daring you to notice the incongruity of each other -
His shirt sleeves squeezed to the stitches,
Holding a bright red leash.
So much arm for so little pooch.

He walks tall and stares down anyone approaching him,
Dreadlocked and bejeaned,
Tattooed and doc martined.
He was known as Cannabis Chris.
No one knew his real name -
A doobey in one hand, leash in the other.
His gratuity made him profoundly unarrestable.

He'd knock on your door on his way to the park,
Demand a zecspresso, three heaped spoons of nescafe and
    a small amount of hot water
Then he'd sit in your living room, spark up the strongest
    joint you'd ever had -
Skunk and solid with a bit of herbal tobacco.
All mixed up like your head was gonna be

Your house was so fogged up that the housemates on the
    top floor were high without leaving their rooms.
As he told you of his escapades and scrapes you'd be rolling
    around on the floor.

Curled up in the foetal position just to stop the world from
    spinning.
Then he'd finish his drink,
Stub out his spliff,
And leave

To carry on to the park,
With his tiny dog,
Staring down the normal folk who dare to question.
With his gravel scraped vocal chords, he'd call back his
    dog,
Shouting at the top of his croaky voice
"Tinkerbell!" "Tinksie, get back!"

Yard

You can be a mouse in a field, quietly eating some grain
Or the buzzard circling overhead waiting to pounce
Or the onlooker eating his lunch, admiring the scene:
One of us will soon be dead,
The other two satisfyingly satiated

This place, this dead piece of land
Left to be filled with waste from folks gardens.
This awkwardly placed farmland between a bijou barn and
    guest house
Where benches have been made -
Logs to warm the hearts and houses under the downs
where the logs have been cut and split and stacked and
    stored
Waiting to be moved and moved and moved and burnt
Where compost and mulch slowly heats and decomposes
The tranquillity occasionally broken by the sound of JCBs
and tractors dropping off something until it's needed again.
The jays and the crows and the tits and the buzzards
The occasional red kite and the out of place pigeon.
The constant sounds of the country.

So much has it seen and heard,
Poems have been written and limbs have been damaged -
The perfect hideaway for a wandering mind,
The perfect place for a mouse to eat its grain

The perfect place for the buzzard to circle
The perfect place for me to eat my lunch and watch

I'd like to write you a poem

Id like to write you a poem,
But I'm struggling to find to words:
How do I sum up one third of our life?
The person who's made me who I am

I'd like to write you a poem,
But I doubt I can do you justice.
Your so much better than a trite poet can write.

Daffodils and tulips are all you need.
No need for a lily or a bird of paradise,
Seeing the beauty in the simplest of flowers,

Sneaking out for a walk and watching the sunset,
Counting the birds as they come to our garden,

Bravely confronting the litter thrower, even though he
    looks like he'd stab you.

You're braver and more honest and more spiritual and
deeper and cleverer and tidier and lovelier and a better
parent and and and and and and

Without you, I'm lost
You complete me

I love watching you dance,
And seeing you smile.

I'd like to write you a poem
And I'll try my very poetest
About how wonderful and beautiful and kind and
thoughtful and strong you are.

But it's hard to write you a poem,
Without talking about how you make me,
How you've been there for me,
From child to man
With patience and love

Together we've grown and changed and multiplied,
yet at the heart is still you.
The woman with the glint in her eye
And fire in her soul
Like a rock in a river
As I gush wildly around you with my stupid dreams.

I want to write you a poem
To make you know how much I care
I'll try and do you justice
But I fear I never can.

Grist to the poetry mill

I walk my dad back to the hotel,
Then walk home alone

Pick up my own kids and move them to their own beds.
He must have done something similar to me
hundreds of times.
To feel their sleeping arms wrap around me and feel their
breath on my neck.
To tuck them in and tell them I love them.
My dad could never do that to me again.
He's not my dad any more,

With his constant repeated questions,
His withered walk,
His whinging and complaining,

His bi-hourly upsets,
Followed by his bi-hourly apologies for getting upset,
His stubborn refusal to move on -
To stay in his mausoleum,
To continue to grieve like she went only last week

Being a shell of the scary old bastard.

When she died, she took away the cunt and left a pathetic
husk

And all we are left with is no mum,
And a completely different dad -

One I have to look after.
One I have to ferry around and look out for.

Before she died, he was a cantankerous bastard
Who isolated and upset anyone that got in his way.
Now he's a pathetic shell of a man
Wallowing

The same questions again and again and again

In my head,
He's better off dead

He just wants to be lying next to her
Waiting to fill the ground and be reunited

It's not even his fault any more
His memory has gone.
It's just the same thing again and again
I understand how he is,
But I just can't stand it.

Walking him home I think about pushing him
In front of a bus.
Or aiming him to the cobbled part of the path
Just to make life easier

For him, of course
Not me

Well....
It's all grist for the poetry mill -
Pile up the shit and make a fucking poem.
But it doesn't even make good poetry
Just vile bile

I go to bed and hide in a darkened room,
Trying to process it all,
Trying to find an upbeat ending -
But there isn't one

The death of an icon

I was only a kid when John Lennon died
Completely unaware of the societal shift
Just sat in North London watching my parents look
    bemused
Amazed that someone so important could be taken
When they were so young.
Just playing with my Lego or hiding in my room,
My whole life ahead of me.
Yet to grow up.
I hadn't hardly started my life.
Yet to discover action force figures.
The ZX spectrum was years away from sending me down a
    path of lost life staring at a screen.
Believing everything my parents said.
Full of hope
Years later, I would sit in the back of the class
Writing the lyrics to Floyd's the Wall,
Alternate words with Alan Tucker.
Years later, Primal Scream will release Screamadelica
And together we would waste the nineties,
Group comedowns on masses of mattresses,
House shares and parties,
Sunday mornings at the big chef, personalised breakfasts
Hair down to our shoulders
40-hour stints
Millennium parties

A cheeky half
Walking to the shops in the morning,
Watching the normal folk go to work,
Knowing we were still going from Friday night
5-hour drives to party in a cottage for two days of buckets
and cauldrons all night.
So few cares in the world.
Falling in love
Talking all night
Never leaving each other's side.
Marrying on a bridge, dancing all night.
All in the time since John Lennon died.

And now David Bowie has died.
And the kids are completely unaware of the societal shift.
They don't seem to realise of what this means
35 years has passed.
Apparently that makes me 44 this year.
I'm in a whole new age bracket.
Feeding the birds and watching them visit.
Occasionally I'll spice up my day with an extra expresso.
Sometimes I can make it beyond midnight if I drink
enough red wine
Sunday mornings mean I can snooze till seven,
Eating salads to keep the midriff under control.
A sneaky watch of BBC news whilst the kids are still in bed
Nagging the kids to have a wee before we go on a drive
Getting up early to beat the traffic for a long drive
Getting a nice bit of steak for tea

And in the mirror is someone who looks like me
But yet he's different. His hair is greyer than it should be
There's certainly less than there should be in places
There's scars that tell stories
A lot of the time he can't get up without making a noise.
What has he become?
His own father really.
Singing the same phrase from a song again and again
Stressing about being late.
Age has found me.
The young seem so feckless.
And they'll never know what it means for
David Bowie to die
Until one day in the future when Bieber is dead.

A poem about mattresses

The mattresses went up and down twice.
Once to be placed on the bed,
The old ones removed downstairs
Via the bathroom to make space as the new ones came up

Then the new ones went down
as the old ones came up,
Via the bathroom to make space

They weren't right,
Weren't comfy
Too fakey.
I don't know
I don't understand

So we wait for the new mattresses to come
To be brought upstairs
Whilst the old ones get taken downstairs
Via the bathroom to make space

This thing, that not even she will sleep on
Wasn't right
So we will make it right

Her standards are so high
Things have to be right

To make it so perfect
To make it lovely

And she'll be right.
They will be right
They will be perfect

Me?
I'dve kept the sodding things.
Once the first mattress was in
I couldn't be arsed to do it all over again

But I'll drag em up and down and down and up
 via the bathroom to make space and into the spare room,
Wherever they need to go.
Cos she's right
It'll be nice
 it'll be perfect

Her standards for perfection are impeccable
So admirable.
Things are nice when they're right

Me?
If it lands mainly flat and not too much in the way,
Then that's fine by me
I'll step over it for the rest of my life rather than
Perfect its position

Her standards are so high
That an egg had to be just right
And sausages?
Where do we start on sausages?
Boston.
That's where we start on sausages
And end

Me?
How can someone with such high standards be with me?
For so long?
I'm no Boston sausage.
Hardly the perfect fried egg.
I had a mild panic attack losing half the family whilst
buying two mattresses, which came up and down twice
Via the bathroom to make space

I knew from that first crazy night
As we kaleidoscoped on a ride
As we talked and never left each other's side
And all these years later, two thirds the life of a cat,
I can see her walk along in a hat
And I smile and see that wonderful being
Who's made me happy
Who's taught me to appreciate it being right.
To love the life we have

This life that we've made together
With two lives we've made together

Wouldn't be anywhere near perfect with just me.
She's allowed me to grow, to morph, to be.
And she's still the same beautiful person I met
On a sofa all those years ago
The same person whose blossomed
And grown

Me?
I'dve never bought the mattresses in the first place.

Sitting cross legged on the floor

Is so easy nowadays
To care and complain
Moaning about being a minority
In a world full of pain

A quick click away
From what I want to say

It's just me and my -insert amount- of friends I have on
Facebook now
Complaining about the government and how
They're making it bad
And how it's making me sad

Vent my spleen
to the people who mean
The most to me
Feel the same as me
Share my views
on the news
Or hate this or that
Or think Cameron's a prat

Sitting cross legged on the floor
In a room full of chairs
Shouting together about how

We're the only ones who really care.

But what good did it do?
As everyone else voted blue.

So I'll keep posting
and liking
and sharing
and complaining

But what good will it do?
There won't be a coup
Or Herbert won't vote
for the things that I hope.

But I look round and see
everyone else seems like me
My news feed is full
of words that seem true
Of pointing out the fucking obvious
Who could not even think like this?
Why would anyone even disagree
with what we can all see?

But it's all so pointless -
so fucking banal and a waste of time,
like banging your head against a big blunt wall:
it just hurts
it's just blood-letting

Just making myself feel better.
But I don't feel better -
I'm just wasting my time

there is no point

No point at all
I'm just sitting cross legged on the floor
In a room full of chairs

But what else can I do?
I only have so few
Resources
My time is filled with work and kids
And playing on my phone
And sleeping and stuff.
All I have time for is too little time
So all I can do is post and share

But what if we all got together
To try and make the world a little better
By passing on information
To all my friends around the nation?
With a quick click I can show my friends
There's a light at the end
A different view
Something new
And we all can agree
To try and be happy

And we can all push away the chairs
And sit down in a circle
And hold a space
And make the world a better place.

Stu

Of all the people at your funeral, and there were more than
I'd ever seen...
Of all the people at your funeral, they all would have
answered your ring.

If only you'd phoned.
I'd be there in a second.

Picked you up.
Put you in my car.
Brought you home.

I was one of so many.
Any one of us would've done it.
But you didn't ring.
Couldn't bring yourself to do it.
Look

Of all the people at your funeral, so few of them knew.
All the people at your funeral would have tried to save you.
You had so many there.
Most of them better friends than I ever had been.
And I would've folded time to keep you around.

But I didn't find out till 8 hours too late.

Can't do anything now.
You're gone.
You could've written a song about it.
Written a sodding poem. That might've helped.

All I can hear is your giggle.
As I was getting ready for your funeral.

YOUR FUCKING FUNERAL, STU!

All I could hear was your giggle.
As I was getting annoyed, I know you'd have seen me and
giggled and I know it wouldn't have been worth getting
annoyed about.

But your giggle is worthless now.

I can't let you giggle away what's happened now.
Because you haven't got any giggle left to stop it.
Maybe that's what I can get from this.
But to be honest, Stu, I'd rather know you were around

I'm not anything

I'm not anything
I don't feel any pain
I don't represent anyone

I'm not prepared to die
I don't want to cry

What have we done?
What have we become?

I'm not a Jew
I'm not a Christian
I'm not a Muslim or a Sikh or a Ba'hai or a Buddhist
or an agnostic or an atheist

How could you pull the trigger?
In the name of whoever?

To kill and kill and kill and kill and kill and kill and kill
    and kill
And then end it all

Who are you?
To do what you do
To feel so much hatred and pain?
To kill again and again?

Whose god?
Who's good?
What makes you right?
Why must you fight?

I'm not west
I'm not east, I'm not south, I'm not north.
I'm not fucking anything.

What makes you so angry
To do what you do?
What makes you right
To do what you do?
What have we done
For you to do what you do?

I'm not wrong
I'm not right, I'm not afraid, I'm not angry, I'm not sad,
I'm not scared, I'm not anything.

I wasn't there
I'm not even sure I care
But now it's done
I'm not anyone.

A star wars t

Out of bounds, Rustington
Legoland, Windsor
Butlins, Bognor Regis
Middle sodding Farm

Staring into my phone,
Trying to block out the drone
Of these mindless clones.
How long till home?

I need the loo
I need a poo
I've lost my shoe
I want the one that's blue

A Friday night
 in the school theatre
Watching thirty seconds
 of shit on a viola

Awards for mediocrity
Whilst wearing a Star Wars T
Space jam on a Sunday.
This isn't a fun day

Footy Saturday morn
Me suppressing a yawn
It's all so boring.
Good help my brain

I need the loo
I need a poo
I've lost my shoe
I want the one that's blue

I used to dream
I used to read
I need to breathe
I need to succeed

Sunday morning in bed
Listening to Radio 4 instead

Running the touchline
The star starts to shine

Reading a word
Recognising a bird

Building a fire
Looking inspired

Brings a smile to your face
Puts it all into place

Let's find a loo
Lets go for a poo
We'll find your shoe
We'll get the one that's blue.

My yin yang kin

My yin yang kin:
Two peas in opposite pods
The fighter and the flow-er -
Born of the same love
Just a few years apart

Cliffs at the coast,
One raised high and immovable, steadfast and strong
One flowing in and out, with hidden depths and full of
    Wonder.

A Viking and a Jew;
The Viking, fair and fresh
Storming in and forcing his will on you.
The Jew, dark and joking
Trying to fit in and keeping everyone amused.

The children a metaphor for their parents -
Without one there wouldn't be the other -
Here to teach us all to get along
And combine to make a new breed.

An ode to the alt-right

I'm a Jew and a cuckold,
A feminist and a lefty.
Your worst fucking nightmare

Your pathetic attempt at Nazism
Is just lunatic ramblings of a dying creed.
You're outdated and unfounded

You can hide behind the dark web,
Wanking each other off with your ideologies
But once it's been seen, all is disgusting

How anyone with a brain could believe it I don't know.
Just because you feel validated by a president doesn't mean
    it will win
You're the dying embers of a fire
Waiting to be pissed on for the last remnants of warmth to
    dissipate and be blown into the wind and disappear
    forever.

My family were out fighting the Blackshirts,
Fighting Powell's little shits
The Rivers of Blood was dammed up and dried out.
Your resurgence isn't even a drop of blood in the Dead Sea.
Just because you huddle together online
Putting parenthesis (that's brackets to you) around Jews'

    names
And trolling and conspirifying
Doesn't mean you'll actually succeed.
Because there's more of us
And the more you piss us off
The more we'll fight you

You don't need love to change you
You don't need re-educating
You don't need mocking
You don't need to be fought
You need to just go away

You can change your name
But you can't change your spots
Alt-right, my arse
You're all a bunch of cunts.

A ghost story

I get up and she's there.
I say good morning, have a cry.
She watches me brush my slowly decaying teeth.
As I get myself dressed, she hears me groan and creek
Complaining about the pain.
Sighing down the stairs, she makes sure I don't make
    myself trip.
Her presence and my fear stop me falling.

Chris Evans' cheerful tones remind me of Wogans past.
A friendly voice waking me up replaced by an alien youth.
I complain to her about him.
But, for the 2,565th time, she says nothing.
Silently tolerating me.

I know she disapproves of me like this
But I don't care
She can't leave
She had no choice
She had no right
She had no way
So I stay
My life shrinking
Getting darker as my eyesight slowly degenerates.
So she remains
With a look of disdain and pity

But she should have thought about that before she died.

The friends and family don't ring so much,
Don't visit so much.
I pretend to not remember these things.
But in my heart I know
But if I go then she goes -
And if she goes, I'll have nothing left
Just a hole in my heart
Shaped like the plain wooden coffin
Buried in the ground
with a space next to it that I'm too scared to get into.

My mausoleum
My museum
My world

Going to build myself a model village

I'm going to build myself a model village
Replicate my world
Going to create a microcosm
Be the king of all I survey

I'll use tiny little bricks to build the tiny little houses,
Mini putty for the windows,
Carefully cultivated bonsai for the trees

This world will be perfect -
No need for any jails
They'll be turned into co-operative seed shares
And fair trade coffee shops and art house cinemas

Police cars will be turned into ice cream vans
Policemen will become clowns

The hospitals will have free parking
And will be free access to one and all

Food will be fairly priced
Sourced from my neighbouring mini farms.
I can pick up the crops and distribute them -
No air miles at all

I'll make the mini people -

Build them from putty, glue and paint,
Be perfect model citizens
From every corner of the world.
All the tiny people doing whatever that they want
Making my model model village run peacefully along

And I'll sit towering over my world,
Observing from the side,
Smiling to myself
At the idyll that I've made

The sounds of music, cheer and contentment will fill my
happy little ears
And I'll be idolised for my generosity
Loved for my benevolence
And glorified for my genius and vision

And any model citizen
Not behaving how I like
Will be taken apart and recreated
Made to be perfect again

I won't tolerate divergence from the ethos
Of my perfect peaceful world.
If anyone is racist or homophobic or sexist or anything bad
I'll snap their model heads off,
And bury them in the ground.

If I catch them thinking bad thoughts,

Or reading the wrong type of press,
I'll put them in the compost and let the worms do the rest.

If anyone tries to question my heartfelt protection,
They can leave my little idyll
And be shaped and re made until they see the wisdom of
    my ways.

I'm going to build myself a model village
Replicate my world.
Going to create a microcosm -
Be the king of all I survey.

Me too

Me too
Me too
Me too
The list grew and grew –

Five simple letters
Symbolising pain and fear
That I have never known

These words inflicted by my kind
Upon women of all ages and all colours and all classes.
People I've known since a child, since a teen, since my
twenties, since my thirties, since my forties.
And how many others are out there?
Not brave enough
Not strong enough
Not wanting to say

And is my conscience clear?
Can I be brave enough to say?
That maybe when I was drunk and young.
Tried it on too hard?
Would I write the words to say a different me all those
years ago wouldn't have been so forceful?
I don't know

Maybe the point of all of you
Writing #metoo
It's there to show
That none of us are innocent
And we should all take responsibility for what our society
    has become
What men have done
And how do we move on?
Seeing these damaged human beings
Finally saying the unsayable
Damaged by stupid pathetic men
Like me
Like him
Like all of us
And I'm sorry

My heart droops
At every new #metoo
A friend
A loved one
An acquaintance
With no rhyme or reason

And I feel helpless

Petty bile

As he sits at night, tweeting his petty bile
He distracts us from the real horror:

The underworld wide web has festered a nest for the
    maggots to grow
And together they have risen and empowered a man to lead
    them into war

This appears to be happening in our time
On our watch
And we are helpless to stop it
As we sit safely in this green and pleasant land mocking
    with horror from afar
Arguing over a tiny majority splitting a country
Splitting the parties,
Whilst our NHS is sold,
The housing ladder crumbles,
And the poor drift away down shit creek.

He's taken on the blacks
He's taken on the Mexicans
He's taken on the transgendered
He's taken on the lbgtqs
But so far I'm safe.

Soon it will spread here

Soon we will have to rise up
Soon we will have to fight
And sitting on our arses, we'll not be enough
Sharing with horror,
Tweeting with anger,
Reading another blog post,
Writing words on a phone
To be read on a phone
To be shared on a phone
Will not be enough.

Our ancestors took arms
Will the woked ones be woke enough to actually put a shift
    in?

Living in a mausoleum

I get up and she's there.
I say good morning, have a cry.
She watches me brush my slowly decaying teeth.
As I get myself dressed she hears me groan and creek,
Complaining about the pain,
Sighing down the stairs, she makes sure I don't make
    myself trip,
Her presence and my fear stop me falling.

Chris Evans' cheerful tones remind me of Wogans passed.
A friendly voice waking me up replaced by an alien youth.
I complain to her about him.
But, for the 2,565th time, she says nothing.
Silently tolerating me.

I know she disapproves of me like this,
But I don't care.
She can't leave;
She had no choice
She had no right
She had no way
So I stay,
My life shrinking,
Getting darker as my eyesight slowly degenerates -
So she remains,
With a look of disdain and pity

But she should have thought about that before she died.

The friends and family don't ring so much,
Don't visit so much -
I pretend to not remember these things.
But in my heart I know,
And if I go then she goes,
And if she goes I'll have nothing left -
Just a hole in my heart
Shaped like the plain wooden coffin,
Buried in the ground,
with a space next to it that I'm too scared to get into.

My mausoleum
My museum
My world

What is it? Moasely?

Julie says she wants a poem
And I suppose I should write her one.

Well what do you write about?
For one, she's so tall
I mean, I'm average height for a woman
And she's well above me.

When I was a kid, I wanted a life
Where people would pop round for tea and wine
And we could chat and laugh
And me and mine would hang out with others.
Well Julie's that friend

There might be a knock on the door
And there she is -
The hazy figure behind the smoky glass.
Kettle goes on, pop goes the cork

Ahh, the sound of a cork popping from a bottle -
My Pavlovian heart skips a beat,
Glugging into a large glass.

Julie genuinely seems to be interested
In my pathetic self obsessions,
Mocking me gently

Not letting me get away with it.

And in return, I can mock her ways
She takes on the cheek the abuse me and the wife throw at
    her,
Laughing at our we-told-you-sos.

Cup of tea to start,
Then a cup of coffee,
Despite how far from the edge we live now,
She can always edge a bit closer.

She lives two lives,
And she lives them with a smile.
Neither is easy
And both are so opposite
But she swaps between them with style.

Julie says she wants a poem
And it's taken me a long time to write -
But I suppose it's hard to say the things we all just assume
And turn them into words on a page.

Phil Davis

He never made it Facebook,
this blond haired kid,
the most hedonistic of all us hedonists.
He'll forever be a footnote in our school lives,
however close to him you were,
however you knew him -
We all knew him.

He was a character that shone in the school,
His laid back stonedness stood him out like a gem in the
    river.
He's just the kid with the big grin,
Sneaking off to smokers corner,
For another can before maths.

His memory isn't sullied by selfies and banal updates;
He never lost his hair or went grey.
We'll never briefly connect over children or random found
    photos

I heard about his funeral too late -
Just dropped into conversation at a party.
I missed a phone call from an old school friend and too
    stoned to respond at the time.
I don't know if I would've gone anyway:
Too lost in my early twenties to deal with it,

Too distant from that past to want to get thrown back
    there.
Too scared of my mortality

And now, a quarter of a century later,
His face, unchanged, stares at me from a year book.
He comes back to haunt me

The Real Press

If you enjoyed this book, take a look at the other books we have on our list at www.therealpress.co.uk

Including the new Armada novel with a difference, *Tearagh't*, by the maverick psychologist Craig Newnes.

Or the medieval thriller *Regicide*, by David Boyle, and introducing Peter Abelard as the great detective...

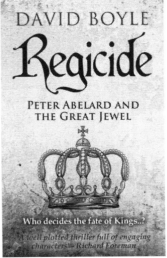